CONTENTS

Dedication of 'Poems'

To *Wilfrid and Alice Meynell*

If the rose in meek duty
   May dedicate humbly
To her grower the beauty
   Wherewith she is comely;
If the mine to the miner
   The jewels that pined in it;
Earth to diviner
   The springs he divined in it;
To the grapes the wine-pitcher
   Their juice that was crushed in it
Viol to its witcher
   The music lay hushed in it;
If the lips may pay Gladness
   In laughters she wakened,
And the heart to its sadness
   Weeping unslakened;
If the hid and sealed coffer
   Whose having not his is,
To the loosers may proffer
   Their finding – here this is;

Their lives if all livers
  To the Life of all living, –
To you, O dear givers,
  I give your own giving!

The Hound of Heaven

I fled Him, down the nights and down the days;
  I fled Him down the arches of the years;
I fled Him, down the labyrinthine ways
  Of my own mind; and in the mist of tears
I hid from Him, and under running laughter.
              Up vistaed hopes I sped;
             And shot, precipitated,
Adown Titanic glooms of chasmèd fears,
  From those strong Feet that followed, followed after
          But with unhurrying chase,
          And unperturbèd pace,
Deliberate speed, majestic instancy,
          They beat – and a Voice beat
          More instant than the Feet –
'All things betray thee, who betrayest Me.'

          I pleaded, outlaw-wise,
By many a hearted casement, curtained red,
  Trellised with intertwining charities;
(For, though I knew His love Who followèd,
          Yet was I sore adread
Lest, having Him, I must have naught beside);
But, if one little casement parted wide,

The gust of His approach would clash it to.
Fear wist not to evade, as Love wist to pursue.
Across the margent of the world I fled,
  And troubled the gold gateways of the stars,
  Smiting for shelter on their clangèd bars;
              Fretted to dulcet jars
And silvern chatter the pale ports o' the moon.
I said to dawn, Be sudden; to eve, Be soon –
  With thy young skiey blossoms heap me over
              From this tremendous Lover:
Float thy vague veil about me, lest He see!
  I tempted all His servitors, but to find
My own betrayal in their constancy,
In faith to Him their fickleness to me,
  Their traitorous trueness, and their loyal deceit.
To all swift things for swiftness did I sue;
  Clung to the whistling mane of every wind.
          But whether they swept, smoothly fleet,
          The long savannahs of the blue;
              Or whether, Thunder-driven,
          They clanged his chariot 'thwart a heaven
Plashy with flying lightnings round the spurn o' their
    feet:–
        Fear wist not to evade as Love wist to pursue.
              Still with unhurrying chase,
              And unperturbèd pace,
          Deliberate speed, majestic instancy,
              Came on the following Feet,
              And a Voice above their beat –

'Naught shelters thee, who wilt not shelter Me.'
I sought no more that after which I strayed
      In face of man or maid;
But still within the little children's eyes
      Seems something, something that replies;
They at least are for *me*, surely for *me*!
I turned me to them very wistfully;
But, just as their young eyes grew sudden fair
      With dawning answers there,
Their angel plucked them from me by the hair.
'Come then, ye other children, Nature's – share
With me' (said I) 'your delicate fellowship;
      Let me greet you lip to lip,
      Let me twine with you caresses,
         Wantoning
      With our Lady-Mother's vagrant tresses,
         Banqueting
      With her in her wind-walled palace,
      Underneath her azured daïs
      Quaffing, as your taintless way is,
         From a chalice
Lucent-weeping out of the dayspring.'
         So it was done:
I in their delicate fellowship was one –
Drew the bolt of Nature's secrecies.
I knew all the swift importings
      On the wilful face of skies;
      I knew how the clouds arise

Spumèd of the wild sea-snortings;
          All that's born or dies
     Rose and drooped with – made them shapers
Of mine own moods, or wailful or divine,
     With them joyed and was bereaven.
     I was heavy with the even,
     When she lit her glimmering tapers
     Round the day's dead sanctities.
     I laughed in the morning's eyes.
I triumphed and I saddened with all weather,
     Heaven and I wept together,
And its sweet tears were salt with mortal mine;
Against the red throb of its sunset-heart
          I laid my own to beat,
          And share-commingling heat;
But not by that, by that, was eased my human smart.
In vain my tears were wet on Heaven's grey cheek.
For ah! we know not what each other says,
     These things and I; in sound *I* speak –
Their sound is but their stir, they speak by silences.
Nature, poor stepdame, cannot slake my drouth;
     Let her, if she would owe me,
Drop yon blue bosom-veil of sky, and show me
     The breasts o' her tenderness:
Never did any milk of hers once bless
          My thirsting mouth.
          Nigh and nigh draws the chase,
          With unperturbèd pace,

Deliberate speed, majestic instancy;
    And past those noisèd Feet
    A voice comes yet more fleet –
'Lo! naught contents thee, who content'st not Me.'

Naked I wait Thy love's uplifted stroke!
My harness piece by piece Thou hast hewn from me,
    And smitten me to my knee;
    I am defenceless utterly.
    I slept, methinks, and woke,
And, slowly gazing, find me stripped in sleep.
In the rash lustihead of my young powers,
    I shook the pillaring hours
And pulled my life upon me; grimed with smears,
I stand amid the dust o' the mounded years –
My mangled youth lies dead beneath the heap.
My days have crackled and gone up in smoke,
Have puffed and burst as sun-starts on a stream.
    Yea, faileth now even dream
The dreamer, and the lute the lutanist;
Even the linked fantasies, in whose blossomy twist
I swung the earth a trinket at my wrist,
Are yielding; cords of all too weak account
For earth with heavy griefs so overplussed.
    Ah! is Thy love indeed
A weed, albeit an amaranthine weed,
Suffering no flowers except its own to mount?
    Ah! must –

Designer infinite! –
Ah! must Thou char the wood ere Thou canst limn with it?
My freshness spent its wavering shower i' the dust;
And now my heart is as a broken fount,
Wherein tear-drippings stagnate, spilt down ever
  From the dank thoughts that shiver
Upon the sighful branches of my mind.
  Such is; what is to be?
The pulp so bitter, how shall taste the rind?
I dimly guess what Time in mists confounds;
Yet ever and anon a trumpet sounds
From the hid battlements of Eternity;
Those shaken mists a space unsettle, then
Round the half-glimpsèd turrets slowly wash again.
  But not ere him who summoneth
  I first have seen, enwound
With glooming robes purpureal, cypress-crowned;
His name I know, and what his trumpet saith.
Whether man's heart or life it be which yields
  Thee harvest, must Thy harvest fields
  Be dunged with rotten death?
   Now of that long pursuit
   Comes on at hand the bruit;
  That Voice is round me like a bursting sea:
   'And is thy earth so marred,
   Shattered in shard on shard?
  Lo, all things fly thee, for thou fliest Me!
8 Strange, piteous, futile thing,

Wherefore should any set thee love apart?
Seeing none but I makes much of naught' (He said),
'And human love needs human meriting:
        How hast thou merited –
Of all man's clotted clay the dingiest clot?
        Alack, thou knowest not
How little worthy of any love thou art!
Whom wilt thou find to love ignoble thee
        Save Me, save only Me?
All which I took from thee I did but take,
        Not for thy harms,
But just that thou might'st seek it in My arms.
        All which thy child's mistake
Fancies as lost, I have stored for thee at home:
        Rise, clasp My hand, and come!'

        Halts by me that footfall;
        Is my gloom, after all,
Shade of His hand, outstretched caressingly?
        'Ah, fondest, blindest, weakest,
        I am He Whom thou seekest!
Thou dravest love from thee, who dravest Me.'

Daisy

Where the thistle lifts a purple crown
 Six foot out of the turf,
And the harebell shakes on the windy hill –
 O the breath of the distant surf! –

The hills look over on the South,
 And southward dreams the sea;
And, with the sea-breeze hand in hand,
 Came innocence and she.

Where 'mid the gorse the raspberry
 Red for the gatherer springs,
Two children did we stray and talk
 Wise, idle, childish things.

She listened with big-lipped surprise,
 Breast-deep 'mid flower and spine:
Her skin was like a grape, whose veins
 Run snow instead of wine.

She knew not those sweet words she spake,
 Nor knew her own sweet way;
But there's never a bird so sweet a song
 Thronged in whose throat that day!

Oh, there were flowers in Storrington
　　On the turf and on the spray;
But the sweetest flower on Sussex hills
　　Was the Daisy-flower that day!

Her beauty smoothed earth's furrowed face!
　　She gave me tokens three:–
A look, a word of her winsome mouth,
　　And a wild raspberry.

A berry red, a guileless look,
　　A still word, – strings of sand!
And yet they made my wild, wild heart
　　Fly down to her little hand.

For, standing artless as the air,
　　And candid as the skies,
She took the berries with her hand,
　　And the love with her sweet eyes.

The fairest things have fleetest end:
　　Their scent survives their close,
But the rose's scent is bitterness
　　To him that loved the rose!

She looked a little wistfully,
　　Then went her sunshine way:–

The sea's eye had a mist on it,
    And the leaves fell from the day.

She went her unremembering way,
    She went, and left in me
The pang of all the partings gone,
    And partings yet to be.

Still, still I seemed to see her, still
    Look up with soft replies,
And take the berries with her hand,
    And the love with her lovely eyes.

Nothing begins, and nothing ends,
    That is not paid with moan;
For we are born in others' pain,
    And perish in our own.

The Making of Viola

The Father of Heaven.   1
>> Spin, daughter Mary, spin,
>>> Twirl your wheel with silver din;
>> Spin, daughter Mary, spin,
>>> Spin a tress for Viola.

Angels.
>> Spin, Queen Mary, a
>> Brown tress for Viola!

The Father of Heaven.   2
>> Weave, hands angelical,
>> Weave a woof of flesh to pall –
>> Weave, hands angelical –
>>> Flesh to pall our Viola.

Angels.
>> Weave, singing brothers, a
>> Velvet flesh for Viola!

The Father of Heaven.   3
>> Scoop, young Jesus, for her eyes,
>> Wood-browned pools of Paradise –
>> Young Jesus, for the eyes,
>>> For the eyes of Viola.

Angels.

> Tint, Prince Jesus, a
> Duskèd eye for Viola!

The Father of Heaven.   4

> Cast a star therein to drown,
> Like a torch in cavern brown,
> Sink a burning star to drown
>   Whelmed in eyes of Viola.

Angels.

> Lave, Prince Jesus, a
> Star in eyes of Viola.

The Father of Heaven.   5

> Breathe, Lord Paraclete,
> To a bubbled crystal meet –
> Breathe, Lord Paraclete –
>   Crystal soul for Viola.

Angels.

> Breathe, Regal Spirit, a
> Flashing soul for Viola!

The Father of Heaven.   6

> Child-angels, from your wings
> Fall the roseal hoverings,

Child-angels, from your wings
On the cheeks of Viola.

Angels.

Linger, rosy reflex, a
Quenchless stain, on Viola!

7

All things being accomplished, saith the Father of Heaven:
Bear her down, and bearing sing,
Bear her down on spyless wing,
Bear her down, and bearing sing,
With a sound of Viola.

Angels.

Music as her name is, a
Sweet sound of Viola!

8

Wheeling angels, past espial,
Danced her down with sound of viola;
Wheeling angels, past espial,
Descanting on 'Viola.'

Angels.

Sing, in our footing, a
Lovely lilt of 'Viola'!

9

Baby smiled, mother wailed,
Earthward while the sweetling sailed;
Mother smiled, baby wailed,
　　When to earth came Viola.
And her elders shall say:
　　So soon have we taught you a
　　Way to weep, poor Viola!

10

Smile, sweet baby, smile,
For you will have weeping-while;
Native in your Heaven is smile, –
　　But your weeping, Viola?

Whence your smiles, we know, but ah!
Whence your weeping, Viola? –
Our first gifts to you is a
Gift of tears, my Viola!

Ex Ore Infantium

Little Jesus, wast Thou shy
Once, and just so small as I?
And what did it feel like to be
Out of Heaven, and just like me?
Didst Thou sometimes think of *there*,
And ask where all the angels were?
I should think that I would cry
For my house all made of sky;
I would look about the air,
And wonder where my angels were;
And at waking 'twould distress me –
Not an angel there to dress me!

Hadst Thou ever any toys,
Like us little girls and boys?
And didst Thou play in Heaven with all
The angels, that were not too tall,
With stars for marbles? Did the things
Play *Can you see me?* through their wings?

Didst Thou kneel at night to pray,
And didst Thou join Thy hands, this way?
And did they tire sometimes, being young,

And make the prayer seem very long?
And dost Thou like it best, that we
Should join our hands to pray to Thee?
I used to think, before I knew,
The prayer not said unless we do.
And did Thy Mother at the night
Kiss Thee, and fold the clothes in right?
And didst Thou feel quite good in bed,
Kissed, and sweet, and Thy prayers said?

Thou canst not have forgotten all
That it feels like to be small:
And Thou know'st I cannot pray
To Thee in my father's way –
When Thou wast so little, say,
Couldst Thou talk Thy Father's way? –
So, a little Child, come down
And hear a child's tongue like Thy own;
Take me by the hand and walk,
And listen to my baby-talk.
To Thy Father show my prayer
(He will look, Thou art so fair),
And say: 'O Father, I, Thy Son,
Bring the prayer of a little one.'

And He will smile, that children's tongue
Has not changed since Thou wast young!

The Child-Woman

O thou most dear!
Who art thy sex's complex harmony
       God-set more facilely;
       To thee may love draw near
       Without one blame or fear,
Unchidden save by his humility:
Thou Perseus' Shield! wherein I view secure
The mirrored Woman's fateful-fair allure!
Whom Heaven still leaves a twofold dignity,
As girlhood gentle, and as boyhood free;
With whom no most diaphanous webs enwind
The bared limbs of the rebukeless mind.
Wild Dryad! all unconscious of thy tree,
       With which indissolubly
The tyrannous Time shall one day make thee whole;
Whose frank arms pass unfettered through its bole:
       Who wear'st thy femineity
Light as entrailèd blossoms, that shalt find
It erelong silver shackles unto thee.
Thou whose young sex is yet but in thy soul; –
       As, hoarded in the vine,
Hang the gold skins of undelirious wine,
As air sleeps, till it toss its limbs in breeze:–

In whom the mystery which lures and sunders,
     Grapples and thrusts apart, endears, estranges,
– The dragon to its own Hesperides –
     Is gated under slow-revolving changes,
Manifold doors of heavy-hinged years.
     So once, ere Heaven's eyes were filled with wonders
          To see Laughter rise from Tears,
          Lay in beauty not yet mighty,
               Conchèd in translucencies,
          The antenatal Aphrodite,
Caved magicaly under magic seas;
Caved dreamlessly beneath the dreamful seas.

          'Whose sex is in thy soul!'
          What think we of thy soul?
          Which has no parts, and cannot grow,
          Unfurled not from an embryo;
Born of full stature, lineal to control;
          And yet a pigmy's yoke must undergo.
Yet must keep pace and tarry, patient, kind,
With its unwilling scholar, the dull, tardy mind;
Must be obsequious to the body's powers,
Whose low hands mete its paths, set ope and close its
ways;
          Must do obeisance to the days,
And wait the little pleasure of the hours;
          Yea, ripe for kingship, yet must be
Captive in statuted minority!
So is all power fulfilled, as soul in thee.

So still the ruler by the ruled takes rule,
And wisdom weaves itself i' the loom o' the fool.
The splendid sun no splendour can display,
Till on gross things he dash his broken ray,
From cloud and tree and flower re-tossed in prismy
    spray.
Did not obstruction's vessel hem it in,
Force were not force, would spill itself in vain;
We know the Titan by his champèd chain;
Stay is heat's cradle, it is rocked therein,
And by cheek's hand is burnished into light;
If hate were none, would love burn lowlier bright?
God's Fair were guessed scarce but for opposite sin;
Yea, and His Mercy, I do think it well,
Is flashed back from the brazen gates of Hell.
          The heavens decree
All power fulfil itself as soul in thee.
For supreme Spirit subject was to clay,
    And Law from its own servants learned a law,
And Light besought a lamp unto its way,
         And Awe was reined in awe,
       At one small house of Nazareth;
       And Golgotha
Saw Breath to breathlessness resign its breath,
And Life do homage for its crown to death.

Before Her Portrait in Youth

As lovers, banished from their lady's face,
         And hopeless of her grace,
Fashion a ghostly sweetness in its place,
                  Fondly adore
Some stealth-won cast attire she wore,
         A kerchief, or a glove:
                  And at the lover's beck
         Into the glove there fleets the hand,
         Or at impetuous command
Up from the kerchief floats the virgin neck:
So I, in very lowlihead of love, –
                  Too shyly reverencing
         To let one thought's light footfall smooth
Tread near the living, consecrated thing, –
         Treasure me thy cast youth.
This outworn vesture, tenantless of thee,
                  Hath yet my knee,
         For that, with show and semblance fair
                  Of the past Her
Who once the beautiful, discarded raiment bare,
                  It cheateth me.
         As gale to gale drifts breath
         Of blossoms' death,

So dropping down the years from hour to hour
    This dead youth's scent is wafted me to-day:
I sit, and from the fragrance dream the flower.
        So, then she looked (I say);
        And so her front sunk down
Heavy beneath the poet's iron crown:
            On her mouth museful sweet –
            (Even as the twin lips meet)
            Did thought and sadness greet:
                Sighs
            In those mournful eyes
        So put on visibilities;
As viewless ether turns, in deep on deep, to dyes.
        Thus, long ago,
She kept her meditative paces slow
Through maiden meads, with waved shadow and gleam
Of locks half-lifted on the winds of dream,
Till love up-caught her to his chariot's glow.
Yet, voluntary, happier Proserpine,
    This drooping flower of youth thou lettest fall
    I, faring in the cockshut-light, astray,
        Find on my 'lated way,
    And stoop, and gather for memorial,
And lay it on my bosom, and make it mine.
To this, the all of love the stars allow me,
        I dedicate and vow me.
        I reach back through the days
A trothed hand to the dead the last trump shall not raise.   23

The water-wraith that cries
From those eternal sorrows of thy pictured eyes
Entwines and draws me down their soundless intricacies!

A Carrier Song

Since you have waned from us,
Fairest of women,
I am a darkened cage
   Song cannot hymn in,
My songs have followed you,
   Like birds the summer;
Ah! bring them back to me,
   Swiftly, dear comer!
      Seraphim,
      Her to hymn,
      Might leave their portals;
      And at my feet learn
      The harping of mortals!

Whereso your angel is,
   My angel goeth;
I am left guardianless,
   Paradise knoweth!
I have no Heaven left
   To weep my wrongs to;
Heaven, when you went from us,
   Went with my songs too.

Seraphim,
Her to hymn,
Might leave their portals;
And at my feet learn
The harping of mortals!

I have no angels left
   Now, Sweet, to pray to:
Where you have made your shrine
   They are away to.
They have struck Heaven's tent,
   And gone to cover you:
Whereso you keep your state
   Heaven is pitched over you!
     Seraphim,
     Her to hymn,
     Might leave their portals;
     And at my feet learn
     The harping of mortals!

She that is Heaven's Queen
   Her title borrows,
For that she, pitiful,
   Beareth our sorrows.
So thou, *Regina mi,*
   Spes infirmorum;
With all our grieving crowned
   Mater dolorum!

> *Seraphim,*
> *Her to hymn,*
> *Might leave their portals;*
> *And at my feet learn*
> *The harping of mortals!*

Yet, envious coveter
   Of other's grieving!
This lonely longing yet
   'Scapeth your reaving.
Cruel to take from a
   Sinner his Heaven!
Think you with contrite smiles
   To be forgiven?
> *Seraphim,*
> *Her to hymn,*
> *Might leave their portals;*
> *And at my feet learn*
> *The harping of mortals!*

Penitent! give me back
   Angels, and Heaven;
Render your stolen self,
   And be forgiven!
How frontier Heaven from you?
   For my soul prays, Sweet,
Still to your face in Heaven,
   Heaven in your face, Sweet!

Seraphim,
Her to hymn,
Might leave their portals;
And at my feet learn
The harping of mortals!

Her Portrait

Oh, but the heavenly grammar did I hold
Of that high speech which angels' tongues turn gold!
So should her deathless beauty take no wrong,
Praised in her own great kindred's fit and cognate tongue.
Or if that language yet with us abode
Which Adam in the garden talked with God!
But our untempered speech descends – poor heirs!
Grimy and rough-cast still from Babel's bricklayers:
Curse on the brutish jargon we inherit,
Strong but to damn, not memorise, a spirit!
A cheek, a lip, a limb, a bosom, they
Move with light ease in speech of working-day;
And women we do use to praise even so.
But here the gates we burst, and to the temple go.
Their praise were her dispraise; who dare, who dare
Adulate the seraphim for their burning hair?
How, if with them I dared, here should I dare it?
How praise the woman, who but know the spirit?
How praise the colour of her eyes, uncaught
While they were coloured with her varying thought?
How her mouth's shape, who only use to know
What tender shape her speech will fit it to?
Or her lips' redness, when their joinèd veil
Song's fervid hand has parted till it wore them pale?

If I would praise her (temerarious if!)
All must be mystery and hieroglyph.
Heaven, which not oft is prodigal of its more
To singers, in their song too great before –
By which the hierarch of large poesy is
Restrained to his one sacred benefice –
Only for her the salutary awe
Relaxes and stern canon of its law;
To her alone concedes pluralities,
In her alone to reconcile agrees
The Muse, the Graces, and the Charities;
To her, who can the trust so well conduct,
To her it gives the use, to us the usufruct.
What of the dear administress then may
I utter, though I spoke her own carved perfect way?
What of her daily gracious converse known,
Whose heavenly despotism must needs dethrone
And subjugate all sweetness but its own?
Deep in my heart subsides the infrequent word,
And there dies slowly throbbing like a wounded bird.
What of her silence, that outsweetens speech?
What of her thoughts, high marks for mine own thoughts to
     reach?
Yet (Chaucer's antique sentence so to turn),
Most gladly will she teach, and gladly learn;
And teaching her, by her enchanting art,
The master threefold learns for all he can impart.
30   Now all is said, and all being said, – aye me!

There yet remains unsaid the very She.
Nay, to conclude (so to conclude I dare),
If of her virtues you evade the snare,
Then for her faults you'll fall in love with her.

Alas, and I have spoken of her Muse –
Her Muse, that died with her auroral dews!
Learn, the wise cherubim from harps of gold
Seduce a trepidating music manifold;
But the superior seraphim do know
None other music but to flame and glow.
So she first lighted on our frosty earth,
A sad musician, of cherubic birth,
Playing to alien ears – which did not prize
The uncomprehended music of the skies –
The exiled airs of her far Paradise.
But soon, from her own harpings taking fire,
In love and light her melodies expire.
Now Heaven affords her, for her silenced hymn,
A double portion of the seraphim.
At the rich odours from her heart that rise,
My soul remembers its lost Paradise,
And antenatal gales blow from Heaven's shores of spice;
I grow essential all, uncloaking me
From this encumbering virility,
And feel the primal sex of heaven and poetry;
And parting from her, in me linger on
Vague snatches of Uranian antiphon.

How to the petty prison could she shrink
Of femineity? – Nay, but I think
In a dear courtesy her spirit would
Woman assume, for grace to womanhood.
Or, votaress to the virgin Sanctitude
Of reticent withdrawal's sweet, courted pale,
She took the cloistral flesh, the sexual veil,
Of her sad, aboriginal sisterhood;
The habit of cloistral flesh which founding Eve indued.

Thus do I know her: but for what men call
Beauty – the loveliness corporeal,
Its most just praise a thing unproper were
To singer or to listener, me or her.
She wears that body but as one indues
A robe, half careless, for it is the use;
Although her soul and it so fair agree,
We sure may, unattaint of heresy,
Conceit it might the soul's begetter be.
The immortal could we cease to contemplate,
The mortal part suggests its every trait.
God laid His fingers on the ivories
Of her pure members as on smoothèd keys,
And there out-breathed her spirit's harmonies.
I'll speak a little proudly: – I disdain
To count the beauty worth my wish or gain,
Which the dull daily fool can covet or obtain.
I do confess the fairness of the spoil,

But from such rivalry it takes a spoil,
For her I'll proudlier speak: – how could it be
That I should praise the gilding on the psaltery?
'Tis not for her to hold that prize a prize,
Or praise much praise, though proudest in its wise,
To which even hopes of merely women rise.
Such strife would to the vanquished laurels yield,
Against *her* suffered to have lost a field.
Herself must with herself be sole compeer,
Unless the people of her distant sphere.
Some gold migration send to melodise the year.

Yet I have felt what terrors may consort
In women's cheeks, the Graces' soft resort;
My hand hath shook at gentle hands' access,
And trembled at the waving of a tress;
My blood known panic fear, and fled dismayed,
Where ladies' eyes have set their ambuscade.
The rustle of a robe hath been to me
The very rattle of love's musketry;
Although my heart hath beat the loud advance,
I have recoiled before a challenging glance,
Proved gay alarms where warlike ribbons dance.
And from it all, this knowledge have I got, –
The whole that others have, is less than they have not;
All which makes other women noted fair,
Unnoted would remain and overshone in her.

How should I gauge what beauty is her dole,
Who cannot see her countenance for her soul,
As birds see not the casement for the sky?
And, as 'tis check they prove its presence by,
I know not of her body till I find
My flight debarred the heaven of her mind.
Hers is the face whence all should copied be,
Did God make replicas of such as she;
Its presence felt by what it does abate,
Because the soul shines through, tempered and mitigate:
Where – as a figure labouring at night
Beside the body of a splendid light –
Dark Time works hidden by its luminousness;
And every line he labours to impress
Turns added beauty, like the veins that run
Athwart a leaf which hangs against the sun.

There regent Melancholy wide controls;
There Earth-and-Heaven-Love play for aureoles;
There Sweetness out of Sadness breaks at fits,
Like bubbles on dark water, or as flits
A sudden silver fin through its deep infinities;
There amorous Thought has sucked pale Fancy's breath,
And Tenderness sits looking towards the lands of death;
There Feeling stills her breathing with her hand,
And Dream from Melancholy part wrests the wand
And on this lady's heart, looked you so deep,
Poor Poetry has rocked himself to sleep:

Upon the heavy blossom of her lips
Hangs the bee Musing; nigh, her lids eclipse
Each half-occulted star beneath that lies;
And in the contemplation of those eyes,
Passionless passion, wild tranquillities.

A Dead Astronomer

(STEPHEN PERRY, S. J.)

Starry amorist, starward gone,
Though art – what thou didst gaze upon!
Passed through thy golden garden's bars,
Thou seest the Gardener of the Stars.
She, about whose moonèd brows
Seven stars make seven glows,
Seven lights for seven woes;
She, like thine own Galaxy,
All lustres in one purity:–
What said'st thou, Astronomer,
When thou didst discover *her*?
When thy hand its tube let fall,
Thou found'st the fairest star of all!

The After Woman

Daughter of the ancient Eve
We know the gifts ye gave – and give.
Who knows the gifts which *you* shall give,
Daughter of the newer Eve?
You, if my soul be augur, you
Shall – O what shall you not, Sweet, do?
The celestial traitress play,
And all mankind to bliss betray;
With sacrosanct cajoleries
And starry treachery of your eyes
Tempt us back to Paradise;
Make heavenly trespass; – ay, press in
Where faint the fledge-foot seraphin!
Blest fool! Be ensign of our wars,
And shame us all to warriors!
Unbanner your bright locks, – advance,
Girl, their gilded puissance
I' the mystic vaward, and draw on
After the lovely gonfalon
Us to out-folly the excess
Of your sweet foolhardiness;
To adventure like intense
Assault against Omnipotence!

Give me song, as She is, new,
Earth should turn in time thereto!
New, and new, and thrice so new,
All old sweets, New Sweet, meant you!
Fair, I had a dream of thee,
When my young heart beat prophecy,
And in apparition elate
Thy little breasts knew waxèd great,
Sister of the Canticle,
And thee for God grown marriageable.
How my desire desired your day,
That, wheeled in rumour on its way,
Shook me thus with presentience! Then
Eden's lopped tree shall shoot again:
For who Christ's eyes shall miss, with those
Eyes for evident nuncios?
Or who be tardy to His call
In your accents augural?
Who shall not feel the Heavens hid
Impend, at tremble of your lid,
And divine advent shine avowed
Under that dim and lucid cloud;
Yea, 'fore the silver apocalypse
Fail, at the unsealing of your lips?
When to love *you* is (O Christ's spouse!)
To love the beauty of His house.
Then come the Isaian days; the old
Shall dream; and our young men behold

Vision – yea, the vision of Thabor-mount,
Which none to other shall recount,
Because in all men's hearts shall be
The seeing and the prophecy.
For ended is the Mystery Play,
When Christ is life, and you the way;
When Egypt's spoils are Israel's right,
And Day fulfils the married arms of Night.

But here my lips are still.
Until
You and the hour shall be revealed,
This song is sung and sung not, and its words are sealed.

Epilogue to
'A Judgement in Heaven'

Virtue may unlock hell, or even
A sin turn in the wards of Heaven,
(As ethics of the text-book go),
So little men of their own deeds know,
Or through the intricate *mêlée*
Guess witherward draws the battle-sway;
So little, if they know the deed,
Discern what therefrom shall succeed.
To wisest moralists 'tis but given
To work rough border-law of Heaven,
Within this narrow life of ours,
These marches 'twixt delimitless Powers.
Is it, if Heaven the future showed,
Is it the all-severest mode
To see ourselves with the eyes of God?
God rather grant, at His assize,
He see us not with our own eyes!

Heaven, which man's generations draws,
Nor deviates into replicas,
Must of as deep diversity
In judgement as creation be.

There is no expeditious road
To pack and label men for God,
And save them by the barrel-load.
Some may perchance, with strange surprise,
Have blundered into Paradise.
In vasty dusk of life abroad,
They fondly thought to err from God,
Nor knew the circle that they trod;
And, wandering all the night about,
Found them at morn where they set out.
Death dawned; Heaven lay in prospect wide:–
Lo! they were standing by His side!

To a Snow-flake

What heart could have thought you? –
Past our devisal
(O filigree petal!)
Fashioned so purely,
Fragilely, surely,
From what Paradisal
Imagineless metal,
Too costly for cost?
Who hammered you, wrought you,
From argentine vapour? –
'God was my shaper.
Passing surmisal,
He hammered, He wrought me,
From curled silver vapour,
To lust of His mind:–
Thou could'st not have thought me
So purely, so palely,
Tinily, surely,
Mightily, frailly,
Insculped and embossed,
With His hammer of wind,
And His graver of frost.'

Lines

To Wilfrid Meynell

O Tree of many branches! One thou hast
Thou barest not, but grafted'st on thee. Now,
Should all men's thunders break on thee, and leave
Thee reft of bough and blossom, that one branch
Shall cling to thee, my Father, Brother, Friend,
Shall cling to thee, until the end of end!

A Counsel of Moderation

On him the unpetitioned heavens descend,
Who heaven on earth proposes not for end;
The perilous and celestial excess
Taking with peace, lacking with thankfulness.
Bliss in extreme befits thee not, until
Thou'rt not extreme in bliss; be equal still:
Sweets to be granted think thyself unmeet
Till thou have learned to hold sweet not too sweet.

This thing not far is he from wise in art
Who teacheth; nor who doth, from wise in heart.

St Monica

At the Cross thy station keeping
With the mournful mother weeping,
Thou, unto the sinless Son,
Weepest for thy sinful one.
Blood and water from His side
Gush; in thee the streams divide:
From thine eyes the one doth start,
But the other from thy heart.

Mary, for thy sinner, see,
To her Sinless mourns with thee:
Could that Son the son not heed,
For whom two such mothers plead?
So thy child had baptism twice,
And the whitest from thine eyes

The floods lift up, lift up their voice,
With a many-watered noise!
Down the centuries fall those sweet
Sobbing waters to our feet,
And our laden air still keeps
Murmur of a Saint that weeps.

Teach us but, to grace our prayers,
Such divinity of tears,–
Earth should be lustrate again
With contrition of that rain:
Till celestial floods o'er rise
The high tops of Paradise.

The Fair Inconstant

Dost thou still hope thou shalt be fair,
   When no more fair to me?
Or those that by thee taken were
   Hold their captivity?
Is this thy confidence? No, no;
Trust it not; it can not be so.

But thou too late, too late shalt find
   'Twas I that made thee fair;
Thy beauties never from thy mind
   But from my loving were;
And those delights that did thee stole
Confessed the vicinage of my soul

The rosy reflex of my heart
   Did thy pale cheek attire;
And what I was, not what thou art,
   Did gazers-on admire.
Go, and too late thou shalt confess
I looked thee into loveliness!

Arab Love Song

The hunched camels of the night
Trouble the bright
And silver waters of the moon.
The Maiden of the Morn will soon
Through Heaven stray and sing,
Star gathering.
Now, while the dark about our loves is strewn,
Light of my dark, blood of my heart, O come!
And night will catch her breath up, and be dumb

Leave thy father, leave thy mother
And thy brother;
Leave the black tents of thy tribe apart!
Am I not thy father and thy brother,
And thy mother?
And thou – what needest with thy tribe's black tents
Who hast the red pavilion of my heart?

The Kingdom of God

'In no strange land'

O World Invisible, we view thee,
O World intangible, we touch thee,
O World unknowable, we know thee,
Inapprehensible, we clutch thee!

Does the fish soar to find the ocean,
The eagle plunge to find the air –
That we ask of the stars in motion
If they have rumour of thee there?

Not where the wheeling systems darken,
And our benumbered conceiving soars! –
The drift of pinions, would we hearken,
Beats at our own clay-shuttered doors.

The angels keep their ancient places;–
Turn but a stone, and start a wing!
'Tis ye, 'tis your estrangèd faces,
That miss the many-splendoured thing.

But (when so sad thou canst not sadder)
Cry; – and upon thy so sore loss
Shall shine the traffic of Jacob's ladder
Pitched betwixt Heaven and Charing Cross.

Yea, in the night, my Soul, my daughter,
Cry, – clinging Heaven by the hems;
And lo, Christ walking on the water,
Not of Genesareth, but Thames!

Envoy

Go, songs, for ended is our brief, sweet play;
  Go, children of swift joy and tardy sorrow!
And some are sung, and that was yesterday,
  And some unsung, and that may be to-morrow.

Go forth; and if it be o'er stony way,
  Old joy can lend what newer grief must borrow:
And it was sweet, and that was yesterday,
  And sweet is sweet, though purchasèd with sorrow.

Go, songs, and come not back from your far way;
  And if men ask you why ye smile and sorrow,
Tell them ye grieve, for your hearts know To-day,
  Tell them ye smile, for your eyes know To-morrow.

A Note on Francis Thompson

Francis Thompson (1859–1907), English poet, born at Preston, Lancashire. A Roman Catholic, he was educated at Ushaw College, near Durham, and afterwards studied medicine at Owens College, Manchester. Failing to take a degree, he went to London. Here he worked in various occupations, until in 1888 he sent two poems to the magazine *Merry England*. These were recognised by Wilfrid Meynell as works of merit. Meynell rescued Thompson from poverty and opium addiction and helped him to publish his first volume of *Poems*, 1893, which was praised by Coventry Patmore in the *Fortnightly Review*. *Sister Songs*, 1895, and *New Poems*, 1897, both gained him recognition as a poet. He also gained a reputation as a prose writer and published *Health and Holiness*, 1905, dealing with the ascetic life; *Essay on Shelley*, 1909; and lives of St Ignatius Loyola, 1909, and John Baptiste de la Salle, 1911. His most famous poem is 'The Hound of Heaven'.

Appreciation

Great poets are obscure for two opposite reasons; now because they are talking about something too large for anyone to understand, and now, again, because they are talking about something too small for anyone else to see. Francis Thompson possessed both these infinities . . . He was describing the evening earth with its mist and fume and fragrance, and represented the whole as rolling upwards like a smoke; then suddenly he called the whole ball of the earth a thurible, and said that some gigantic spirit swung it slowly before God. This is the case of the image too large for comprehension; another instance sticks in my mind of the image which is too small. In one of his poems he says that the abyss between the known and the unknown is bridged by 'Pontifical death.' There are about ten historical and theological puns in that one word. That a priest means a pontiff, that a pontiff means a bridge-maker, that death is certainly a bridge, that death may turn out after all to be a reconciling priest, that at least priest and bridges both attest to the fact that one thing can get separated from another thing – these ideas, and twenty more, are all tacitly concentrated in the word 'Pontifical.' Francis Thompson's poetry, as in the poetry of the universe, you can work infinitely out and out, but yet infinitely in and in. These two infinities are the mark of greatness; and he was a great poet.

G. K. CHESTERTON

Other titles in this series